EASY GUITAR

ADELE 3

ISBN: 978-1-70515-815-9

Visit Hal Leonard Online at
www.halleonard.com

Contact us:
Hal Leonard
7777 West Bluemound Road
Milwaukee, WI 53213
Email: info@halleonard.com

In Europe, contact:
Hal Leonard Europe Limited
42 Wigmore Street
Marylebone, London, W1U 2RY
Email: info@halleonardeurope.com

In Australia, contact:
Hal Leonard Australia Pty. Ltd.
4 Lentara Court
Cheltenham, Victoria, 3192 Australia
Email: info@halleonard.com.au

STRANGERS BY NATURE

WORDS AND MUSIC BY ADELE ADKINS AND LUDWIG GORANSSON

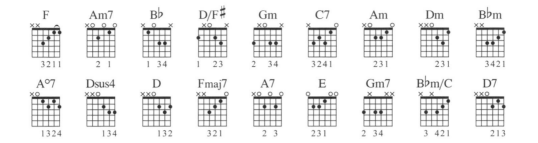

Strum Pattern: 5
Pick Pattern: 3

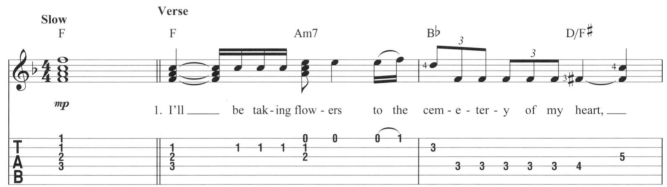

1. I'll ___ be tak-ing flow-ers to the cem-e-ter-y of my heart, ___

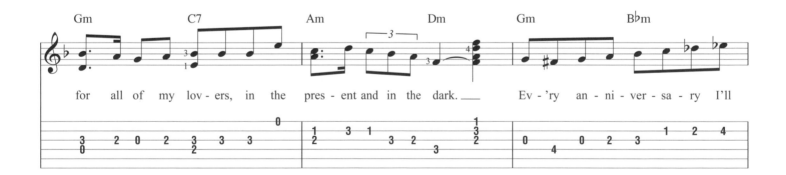

for all of my lov-ers, in the pres-ent and in the dark. ___ Ev-'ry an-ni-ver-sa-ry I'll

pay re-spects and say I'm sor-ry, for they nev-er stood a chance, as if they could, ___ when

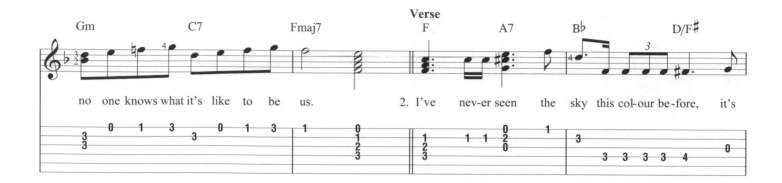

no one knows what it's like to be us.   2. I've nev-er seen   the   sky this col-our be-fore,   it's

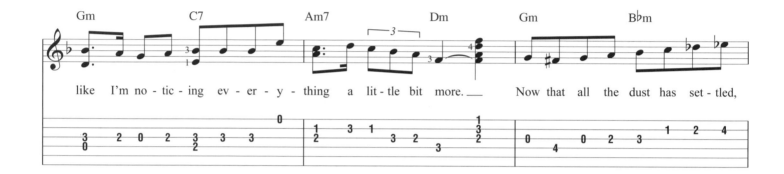

like I'm no - tic - ing ev - er - y - thing   a lit - tle bit more. ___   Now that all   the dust has set - tled,

I   re - but   all my   re - but - tals,   no   one knows what it's   like   to   be   us.

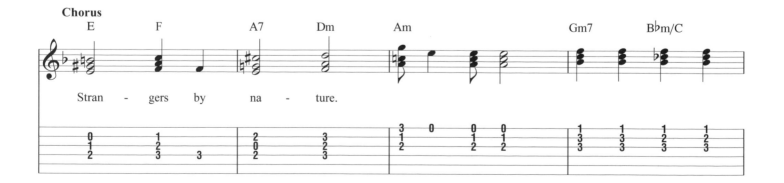

Stran - gers   by   na - ture.

6

Stran - gers by na - ture.

Will I ev - er

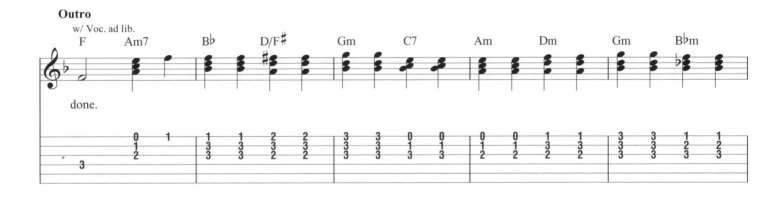

get there? _____ Oh, I hope that some day I'll learn to nur - ture what I've

Outro

w/ Voc. ad lib.

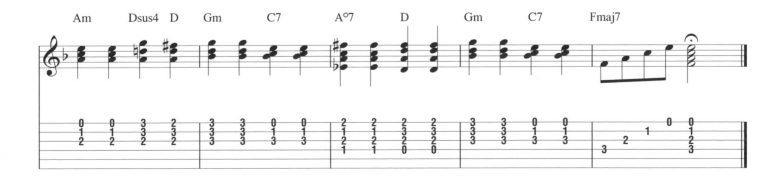

done.

EASY ON ME

WORDS AND MUSIC BY ADELE ADKINS AND GREG KURSTIN

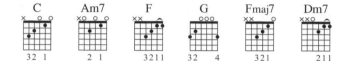

*Capo V

Strum Pattern: 3, 4
Pick Pattern: 3, 4

Intro
Moderately slow, in 2

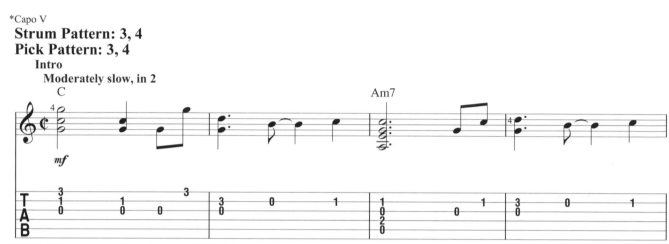

*Optional: To match recording, place capo at fifth fret.

1. There ain't

Verse

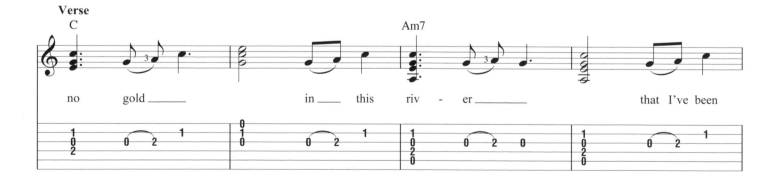

no gold _____ in _____ this riv - er _____ that I've been

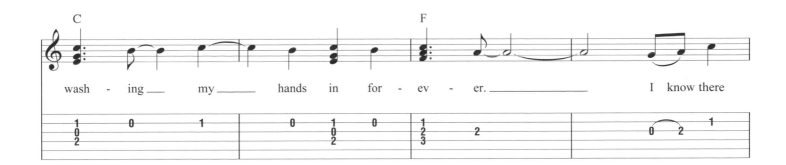

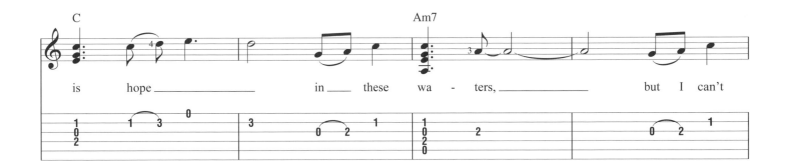

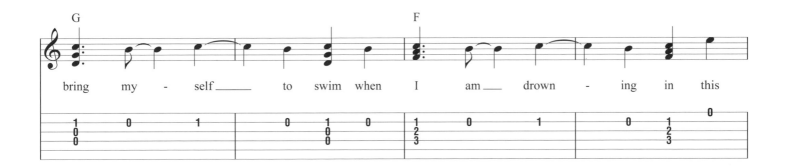

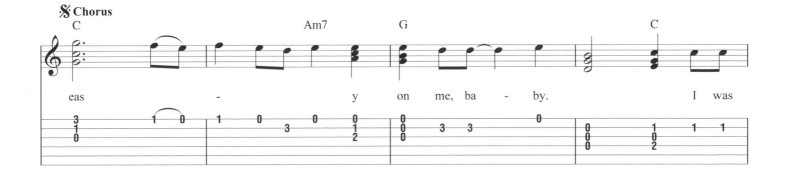

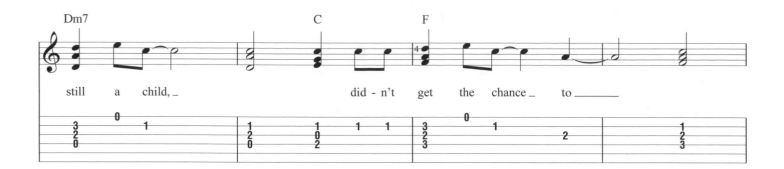

still a child, _ did - n't get the chance _ to _____

feel _____ the world a - round _ me. I had no

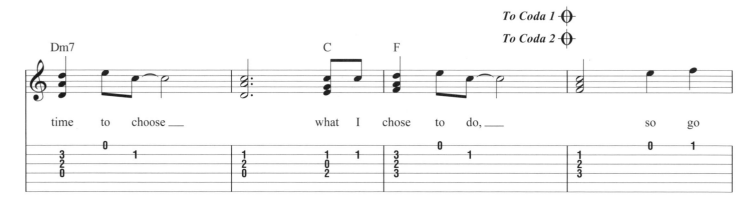

To Coda 1 ⊕
To Coda 2 ⊕

time to choose ___ what I chose to do, ___ so go

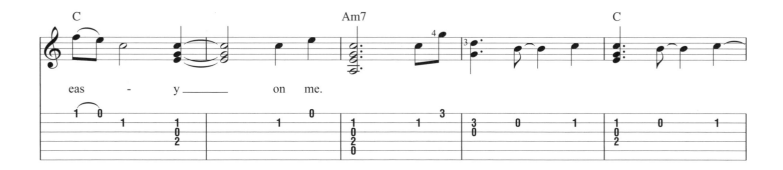

eas - y _____ on me.

Verse

2. There _ ain't no room _____

10

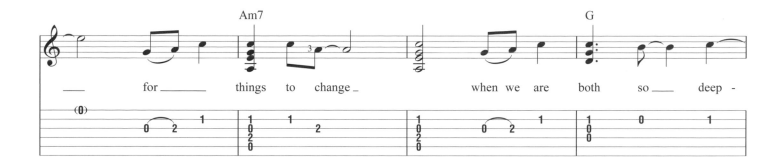

for _____ things to change _____ when we are both so ___ deep -

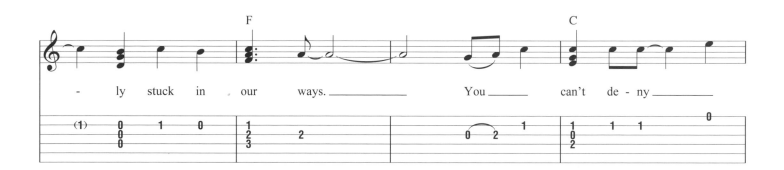

- ly stuck in our ways._____ You_____ can't de - ny_____

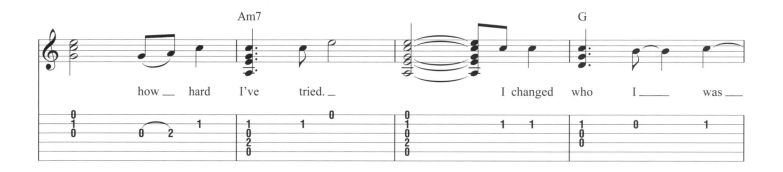

how __ hard I've tried. __ I changed who I ___ was ___

D.S. al Coda 1

_____ to put you both first,_ but ___ now I give up._____ Go

Coda 1

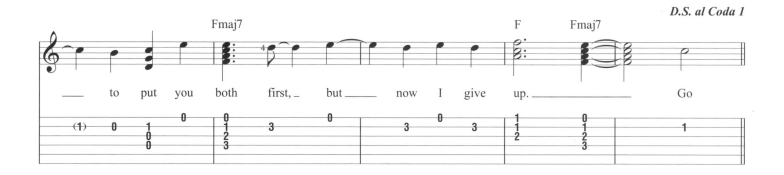

So go eas -

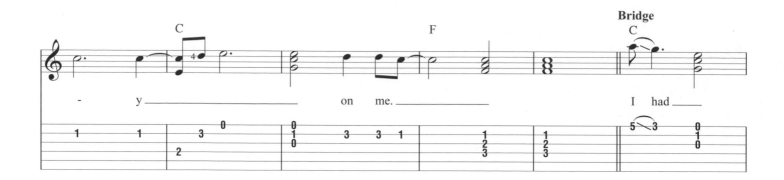

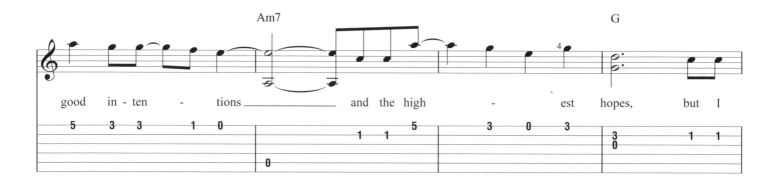

Coda 2

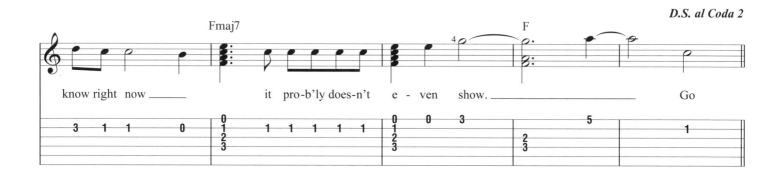

MY LITTLE LOVE

WORDS AND MUSIC BY ADELE ADKINS AND GREG KURSTIN

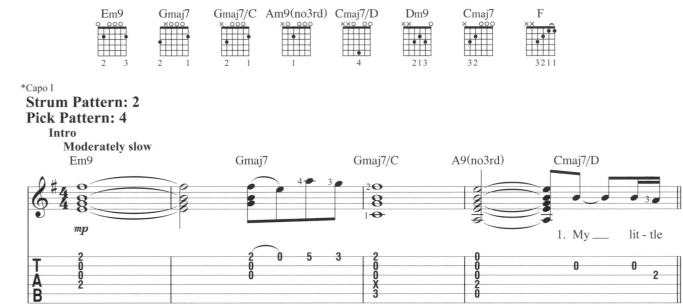

*Capo I

Strum Pattern: 2
Pick Pattern: 4

Intro

Moderately slow

1. My ___ lit - tle

*Optional: To match recording, place capo at 1st fret.

Verse

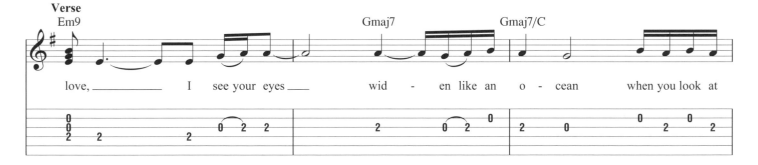

love, ___ I see your eyes ___ wid - en like an o - cean when you look at

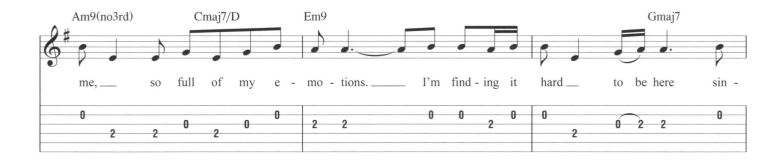

me, ___ so full of my e - mo - tions. ___ I'm find - ing it hard ___ to be here sin -

cere - ly, ___ I know you feel lost; ___ it's my fault ___ com - plete - ly.

13

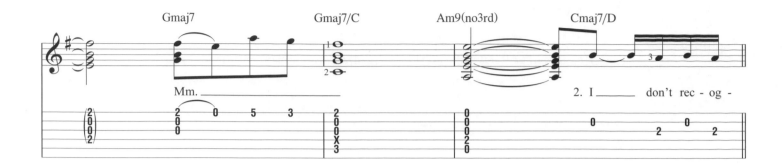

Mm. _____

2. I _____ don't rec - og -

Verse

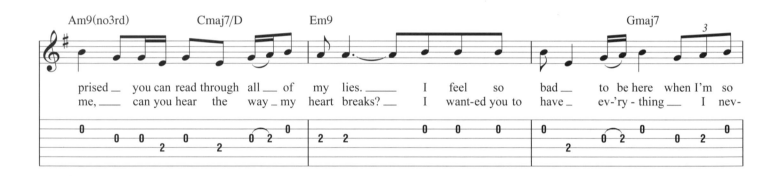

nize _____ my - self in _____ the cold - ness of _ the day - light. _____ So, I ain't sur -
love, _____ tell me do _____ you feel the way _ my past aches? _____ When you lay on

prised _ you can read through all _ of my lies. _____ I feel so bad _ to be here when I'm so
me, _____ can you hear the way _ my heart breaks? _____ I want-ed you to have _ ev-'ry - thing _____ I nev-

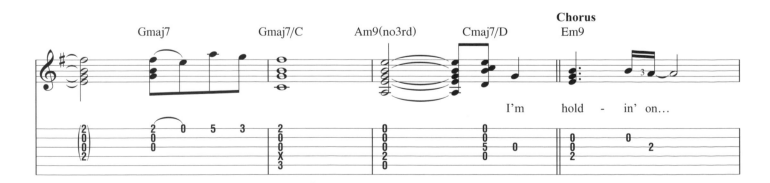

guil - ty. _____ I'm so far gone, _____ and you're the on - ly one who can save me.
er had. _____ I'm so sor - ry _____ if what I've done _ makes _ you feel sad.

Chorus

I'm hold - in' on...

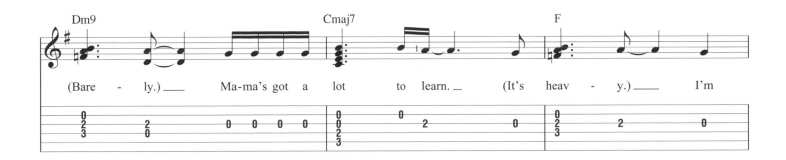

(Bare - ly.) ___ Ma-ma's got a lot to learn. ___ (It's heav - y.) ___ I'm

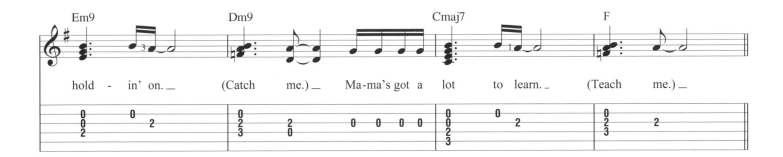

hold - in' on. ___ (Catch me.) ___ Ma-ma's got a lot to learn. ___ (Teach me.) ___

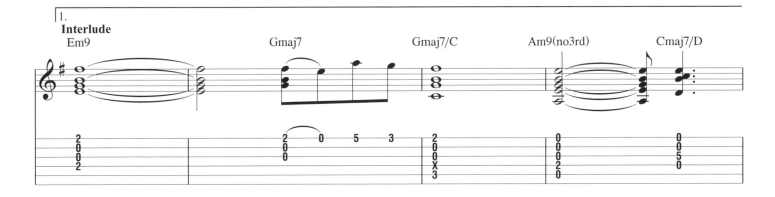

Interlude

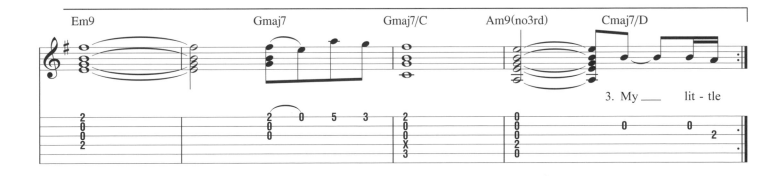

3. My ___ lit - tle

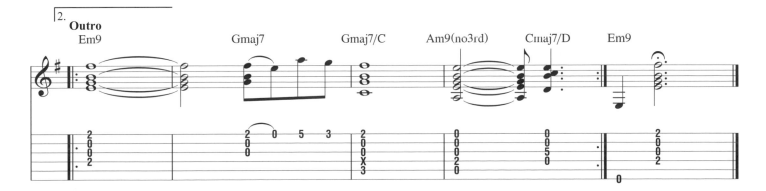

Outro

15

CRY YOUR HEART OUT

WORDS AND MUSIC BY ADELE ADKINS AND GREG KURSTIN

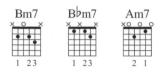

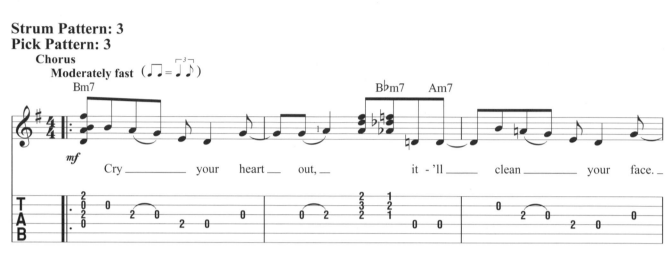

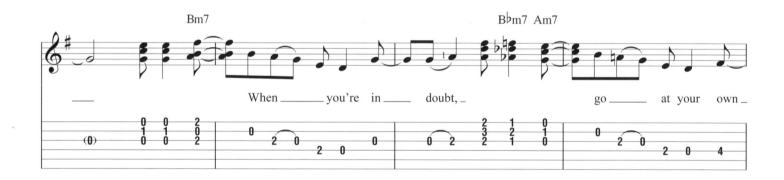

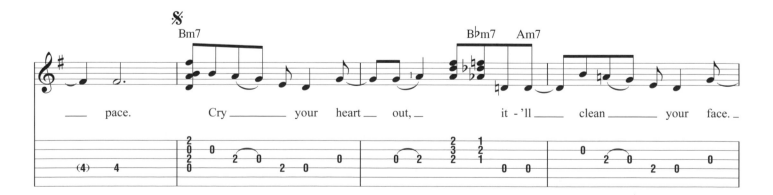

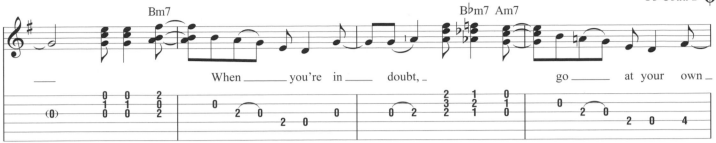

When _____ you're in _____ doubt, ___ go _____ at your own ___

Verse

___ pace. 1. When I _____ walk ___ in a room, ___ I'm in - vis - i - ble, I feel like a ghost. ___
2. *See additional lyrics*

All my friends ___ keep on tell - ing me that this feel - ing won't last, ___ mm.

I can't get no re - lief. ___ I'm so tired ___ of my - self. ___ I swear I'm dead in the _____ eyes. ___

___ I have noth - ing to feel ___ no more, ___ I can't ___ e - ven _____ cry. _____

17

When will I be-gin to feel like me a-gain? I'm hang-ing by a thread.

My skin's pa-per thin. I can't stop wa-ver-ing. I've nev - er been more scared.

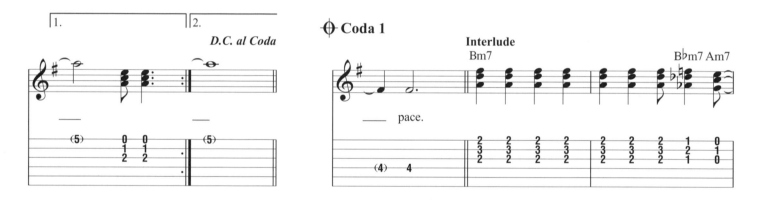

D.C. al Coda

⊕ Coda 1

pace.

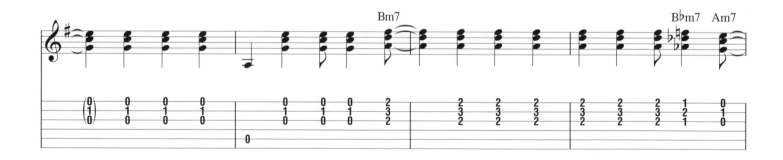

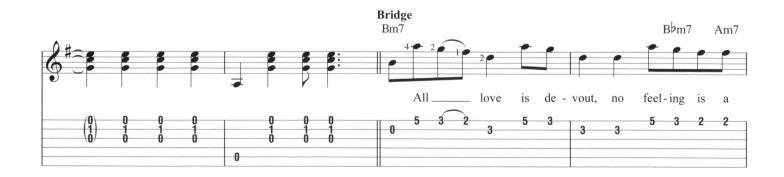

All ___ love is de-vout, no feel-ing is a

18

waste, but keep it to your-self now, be-fore___ it's too late. In the end it's just

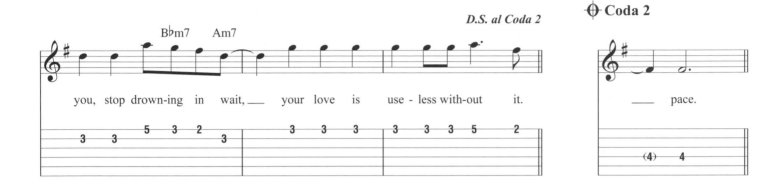

D.S. al Coda 2

Coda 2

you, stop drown-ing in wait,___ your love is use-less with-out it. ___ pace.

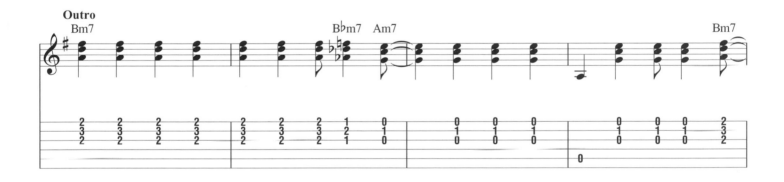

Outro

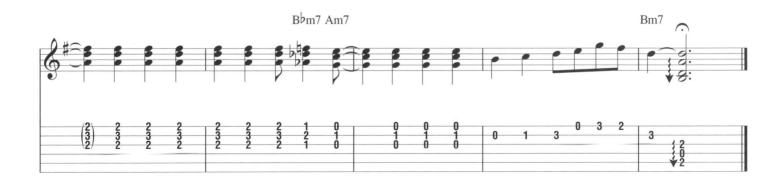

Additional Lyrics

2. When I wake up, I'm afraid of the idea of facing the day.
I would rather stay home on my own, drink it all away.
Please stop calling me; it's exhausting. There's really nothing left to say.
I created this storm, it's only fair I have to sit in its rain.

OH MY GOD

WORDS AND MUSIC BY ADELE ADKINS AND GREG KURSTIN

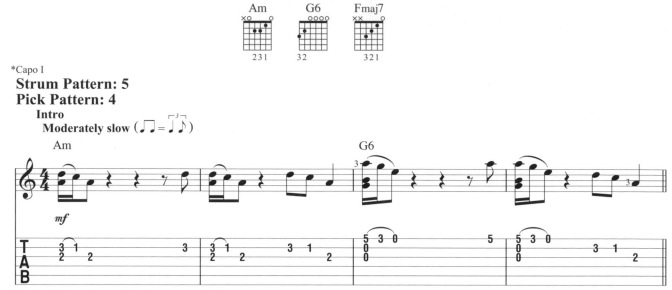

*Capo I

Strum Pattern: 5
Pick Pattern: 4

Intro
Moderately slow

*Optional: To match recording, place capo at 1st fret.

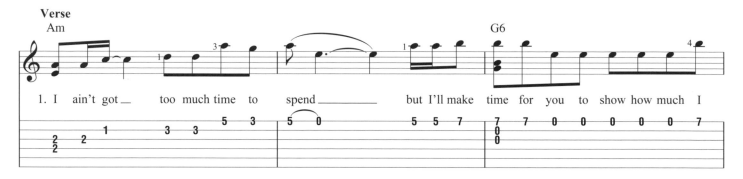

1. I ain't got ___ too much time to spend ___ but I'll make time for you to show how much I care. ___

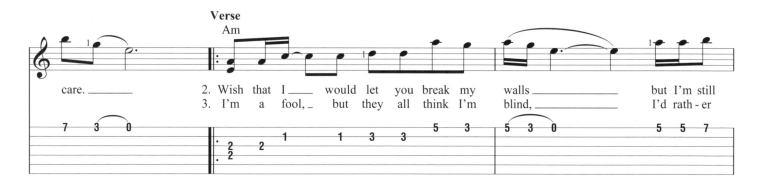

2. Wish that I ___ would let you break my walls ___ but I'm still spin-ning out of con-trol from the fall. ___

Boy, you give ___ good love, I won't

3. I'm a fool, _ but they all think I'm blind, ___ I'd rath-er be a fool than leave my-self be-hind. ___

I don't have _ to ex-plain my-self to

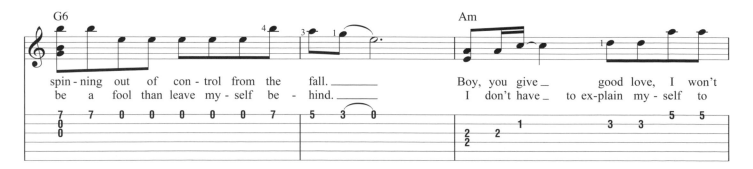

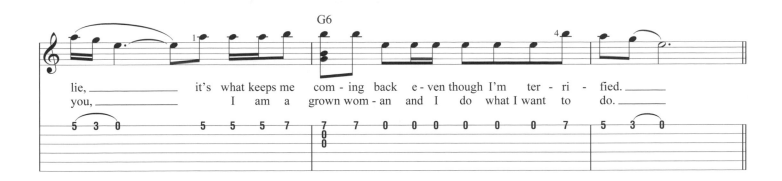

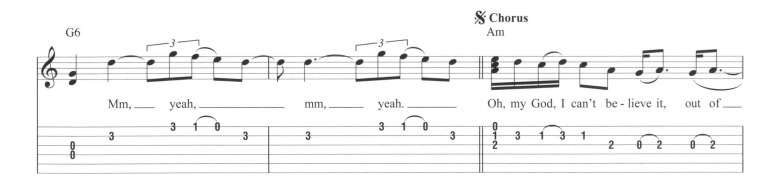

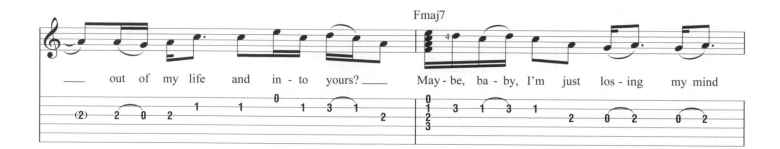

_____ out of my life and in-to yours? _____ May-be, ba-by, I'm just los-ing my mind

'cause this is trou-ble, _____ but it feels right, tee-t'ring on the edge of Heav-en and Hell, _

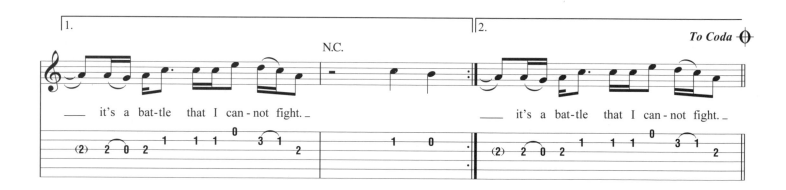

1.
_____ it's a bat-tle that I can-not fight. _

2. **To Coda**
_____ it's a bat-tle that I can-not fight. _

Bridge
Am
Don't let me, I said, don't let me, I said, don't let me, let me down. _

G6
Don't let me, I said, don't let me, I said, don't let me, let me down. _

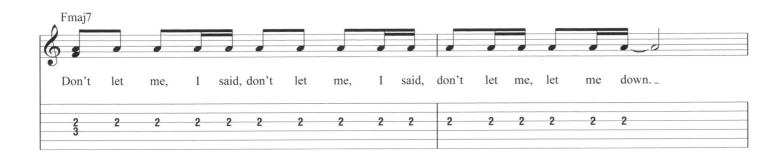

Don't let me, I said, don't let me, I said, don't let me, let me down. __

D.S. al Coda
(take 2nd ending)

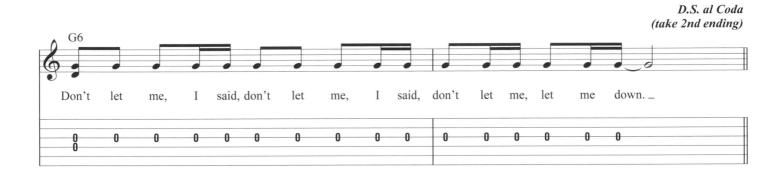

Don't let me, I said, don't let me, I said, don't let me, let me down. __

⊕ Coda
Outro

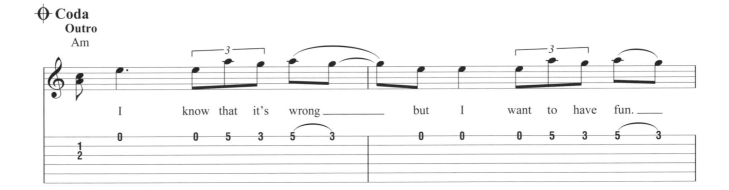

I know that it's wrong _____ but I want to have fun. ____

Mm, __ yeah, _____ mm, _____ yeah. _____ I know that it's wrong ____

___ but I want to have fun. ____ Mm, __ yeah, _____ mm, _____ yeah.

CAN I GET IT

WORDS AND MUSIC BY ADELE ADKINS, SHELLBACK AND MAX MARTIN

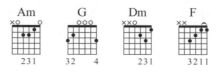

Strum Pattern: 5
Pick Pattern: 4

1. Pave me a path to
2., 3. *See additional lyrics*

fol - low   and I'll tread an - y dan - ger - ous road.   I will beg and I'll steal, I will

bor - row,   if I can make, if I can make your heart my home.   free.

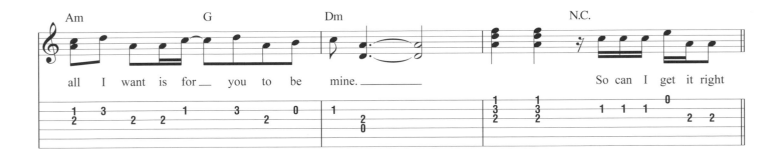

Chorus

25

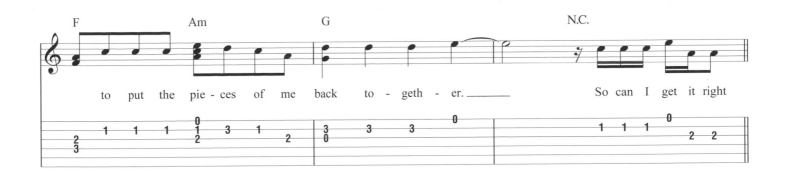

to put the pie - ces of me back to - geth - er._____ So can I get it right

Outro-Chorus

now? __ Can I get it right now?_____

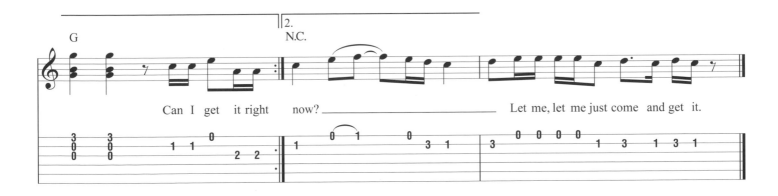

Can I get it right now?_____ Let me, let me just come and get it.

Additional Lyrics

2. Throw me to the water,
   I don't care how deep or shallow
   Because my heart can pound like thunder
   And your love, and your love can set me free.

3. You tease me with your control
   Because I long to live under your spell
   And without your love, I'm hollow.
   I won't make it on my own.

I DRINK WINE

WORDS AND MUSIC BY ADELE ADKINS AND GREG KURSTIN

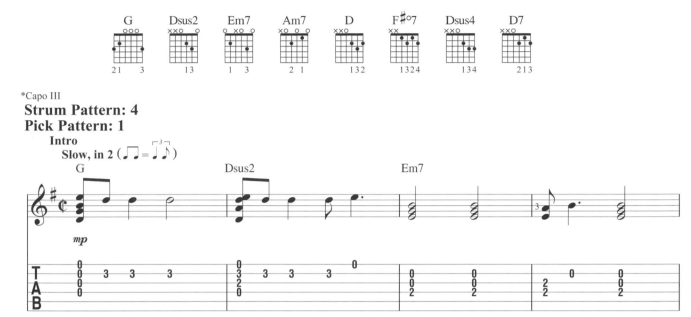

*Capo III

Strum Pattern: 4
Pick Pattern: 1

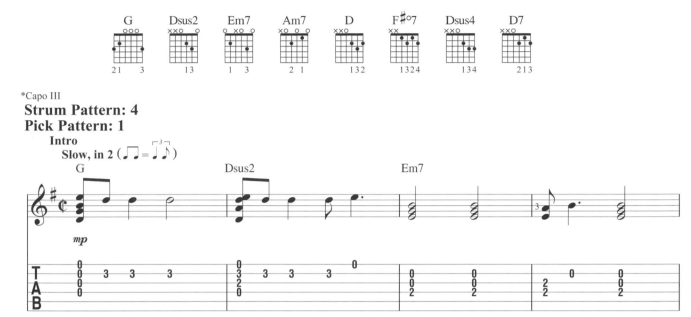

*Optional: To match recording, place capo at 3rd fret.

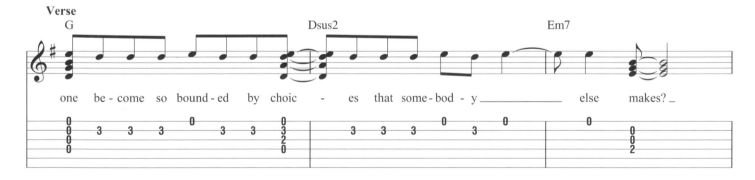

like?   We're in love __ with the world __ but the world __ just wants to __ bring us __

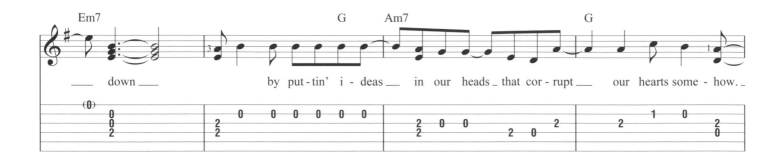

__ down __   by put-tin' i-deas __ in our heads __ that cor-rupt __ our hearts some-how. __

Verse

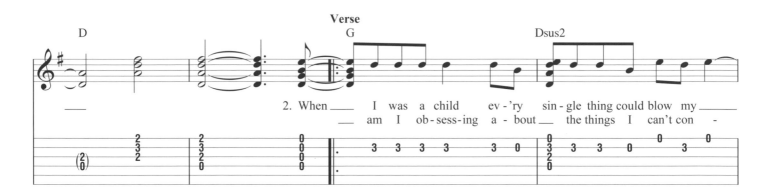

__   2. When __ I was a child ev-'ry sin-gle thing could blow my __
    __ am I ob-sess-ing a-bout __ the things I can't con -

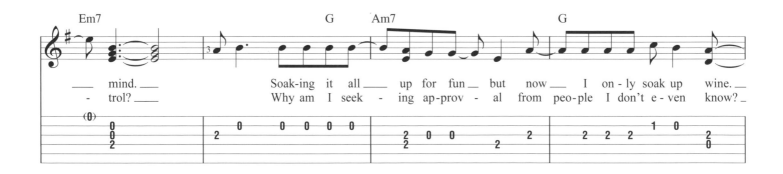

__ mind. __   Soak-ing it all __ up for fun __ but now __ I on-ly soak up wine. __
- trol? __   Why am I seek-ing ap-prov-al from peo-ple I don't e-ven know? __

__   They say to play hard, you work hard, find ba-lance in the sac-ri -
__   In these cra-zy times I hope to find some-thing I can cling on -

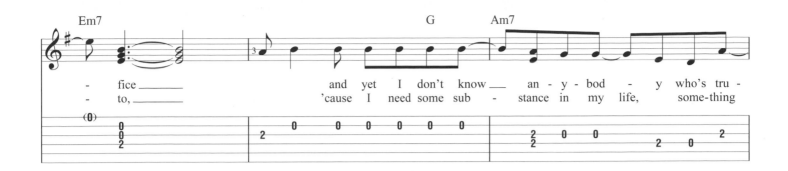

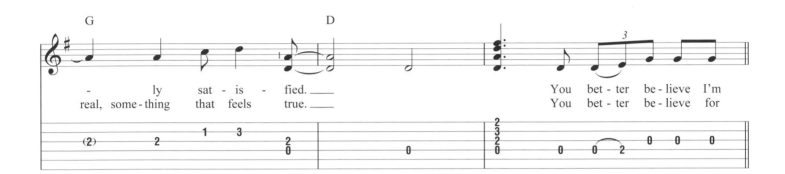

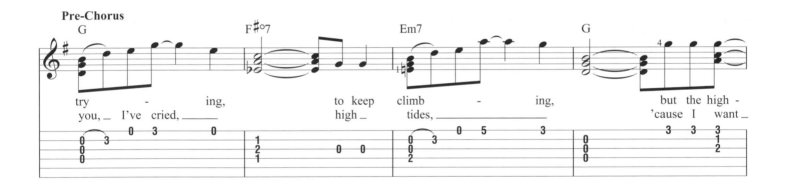

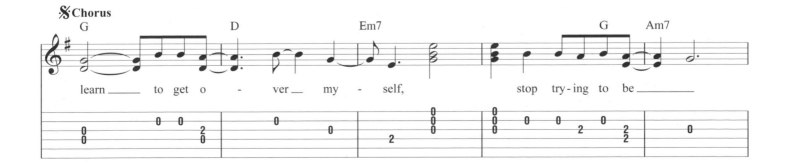

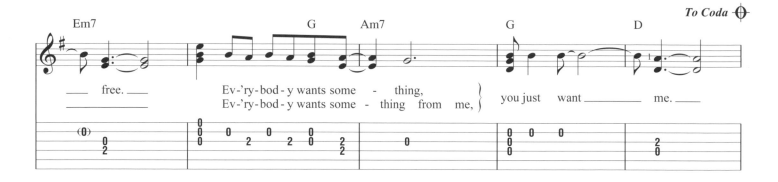

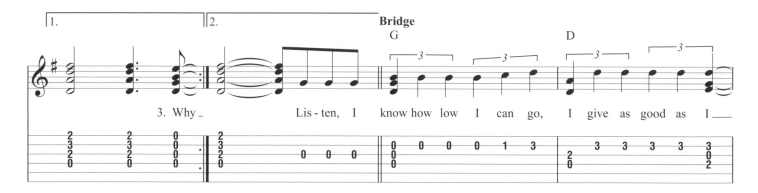

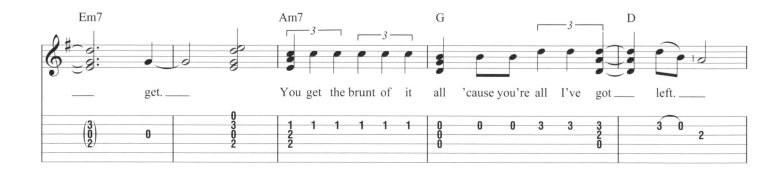

Some-times the road __ less trav-'led is a road best left be - hind. __ Well, I hope I

Coda

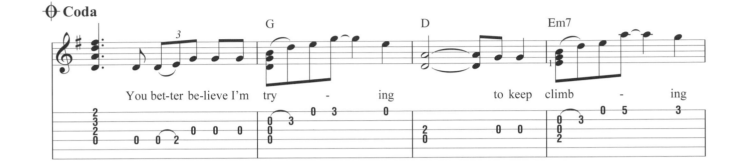

You bet-ter be-lieve I'm try - ing to keep climb - ing

but the high - er we climb _ feels like __ we're both none the wis - er.

Outro

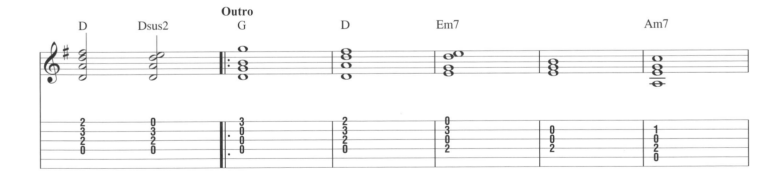

ALL NIGHT PARKING
(INTERLUDE)

WORDS AND MUSIC BY ADELE ADKINS AND ERROLL GARNER

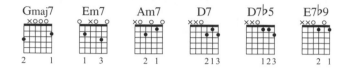

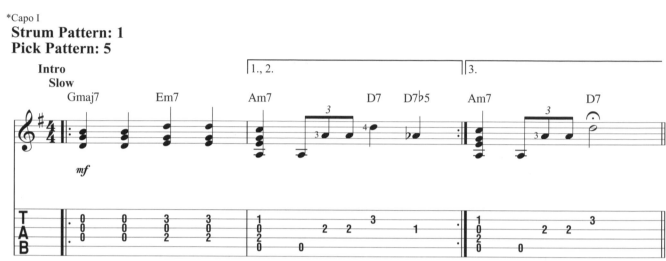

*Capo I

Strum Pattern: 1
Pick Pattern: 5

*Optional: To match recording, place capo at 1st fret.

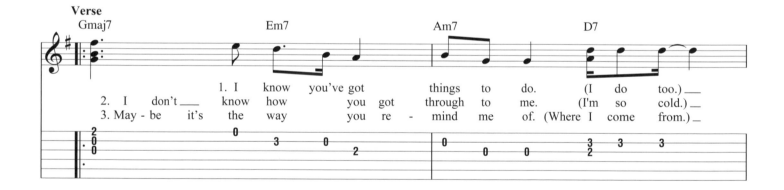

hard to im - press, don't leave me on this stretch a - lone. When I'm
hard to di - gest, us - u - al - ly I'm best a - lone. But ev - 'ry
you is dra - mat - ic, one glimpse and I pan - ic in - side.

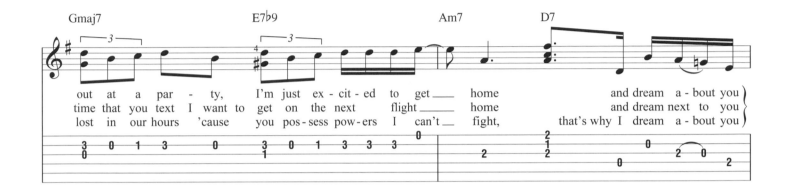

out at a par - ty, I'm just ex - cit - ed to get ___ home and dream a - bout you
time that you text I want to get on the next flight ___ home and dream next to you
lost in our hours 'cause you pos - sess pow - ers I can't ___ fight, that's why I dream a - bout you

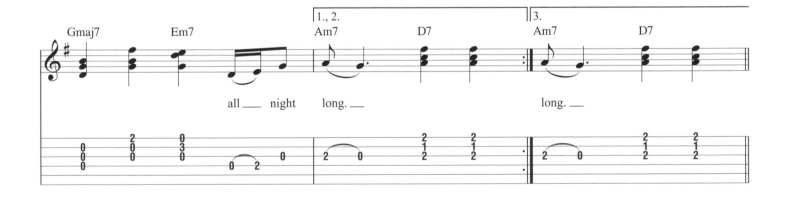

all ___ night long. ___

long. ___

Tag

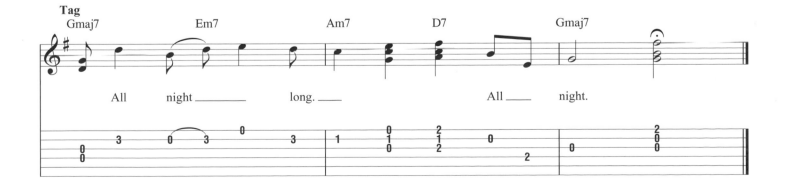

All night _____ long. ___ All ___ night.

35

WOMAN LIKE ME

WORDS AND MUSIC BY ADELE ADKINS AND DEAN JOSIAH COVER

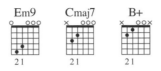

Strum Pattern: 4,6
Pick Pattern: 2, 4

1. You're driv - ing me a - way,_ give me a rea - son to stay._ I want to be

lost in you, but not in this way._ I don't _ think you quite un - der - stand _ who _ you

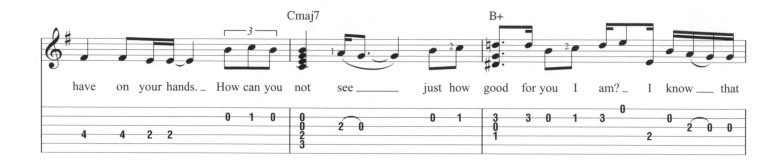

have on your hands. How can you not see _____ just how good for you I am?_ I know __ that

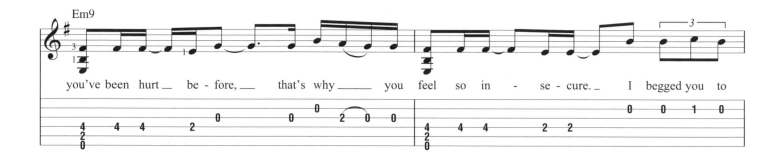

you've been hurt __ be - fore, __ that's why _____ you feel so in - se - cure. __ I begged you to

let me in _____ 'cause I on - ly want to be the cure. If _____ you don't choose to grow, _ we _____ ain't

ev - er gon - na know_ just how good this could be. __ I real - ly hoped that this would go some -

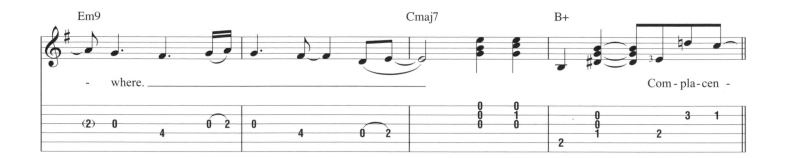

- where. _____ Com - pla - cen -

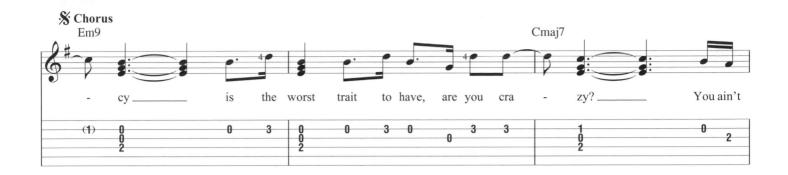

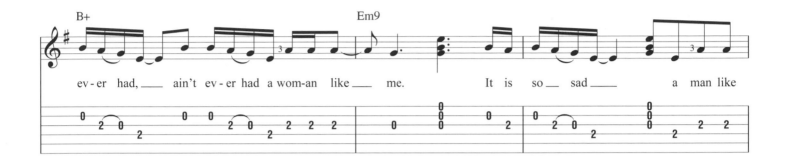

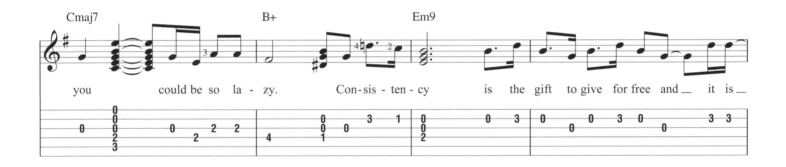

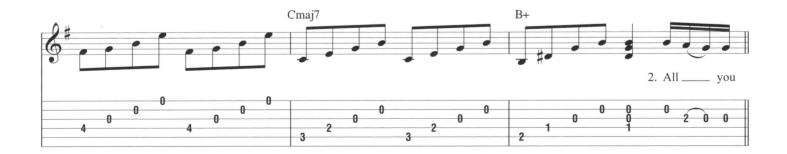

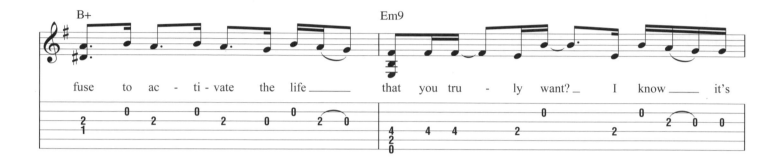

ver - y first time be-cause you asked me to ___ and now you've gone and changed your mind. But lov - ing

you was a ___ break-through, I saw what my heart can real - ly do. ___ Now some oth - er

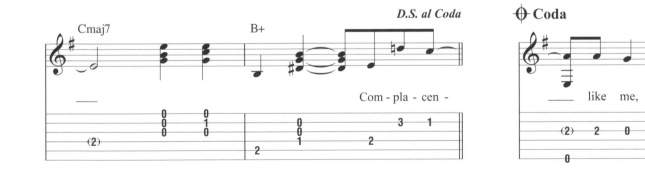

man will get ___ the love I have for you 'cause you don't ___ care. ___ Oh, oh. ___

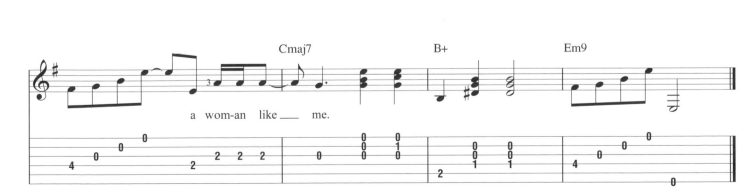

___ Com - pla - cen - ___ like me,

a wom-an like ___ me.

D.S. al Coda   ⊕ **Coda**

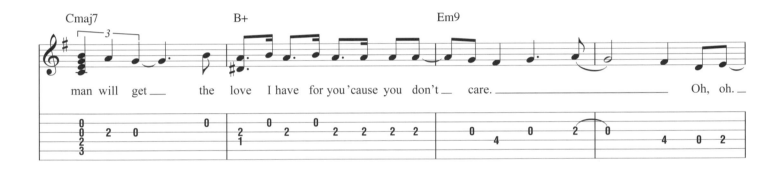

41

HOLD ON

WORDS AND MUSIC BY ADELE ADKINS AND DEAN JOSIAH COVER

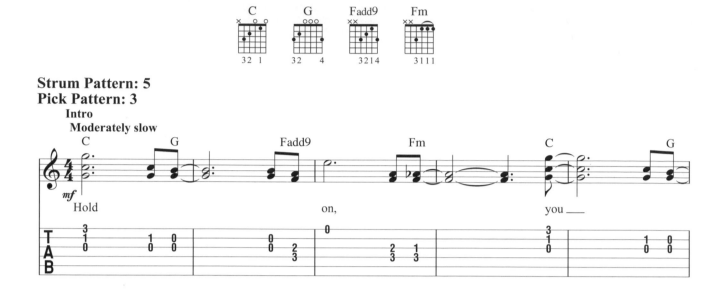

Strum Pattern: 5
Pick Pattern: 3

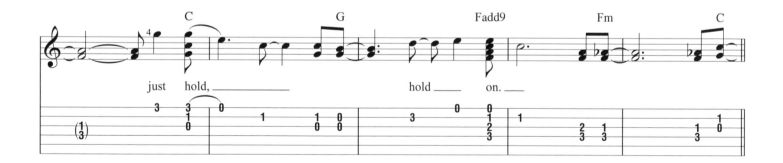

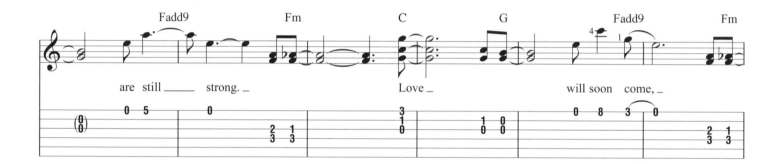

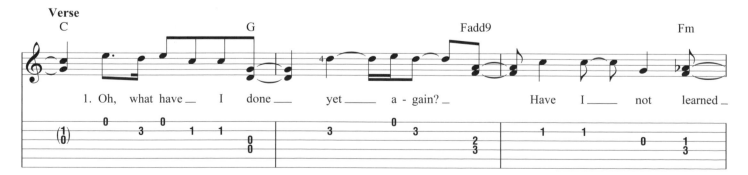

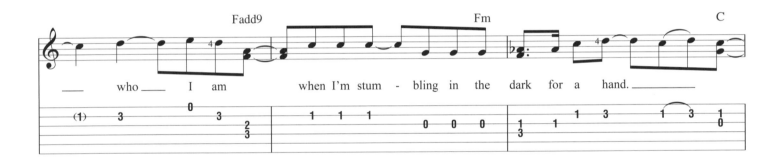

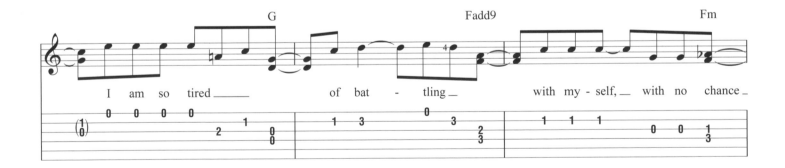

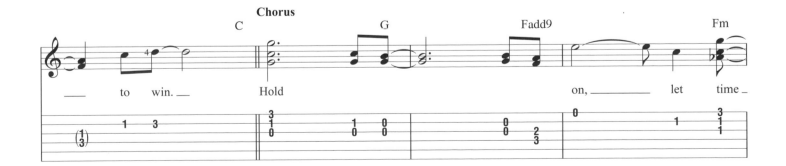

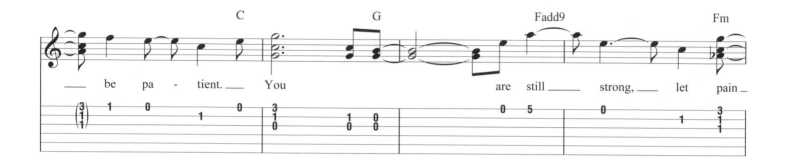

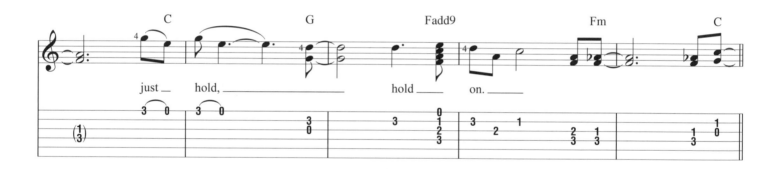

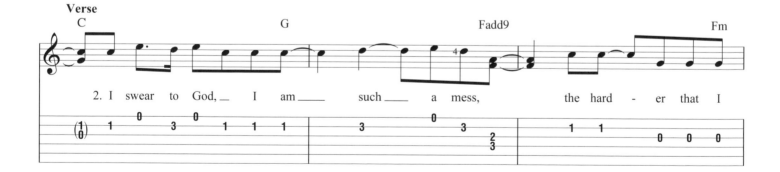

44

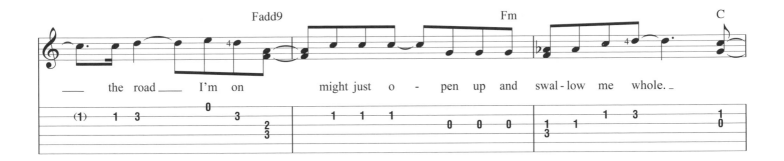

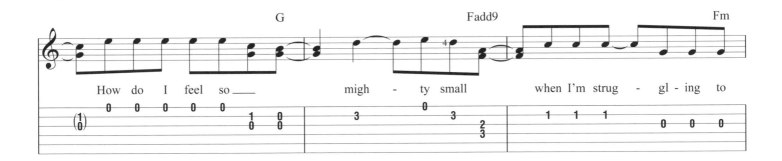

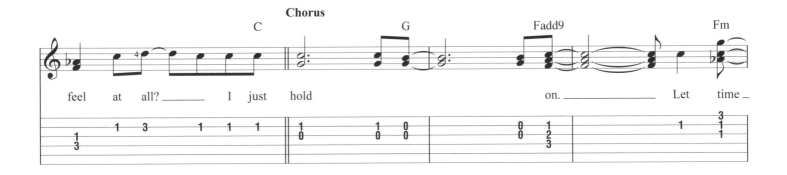

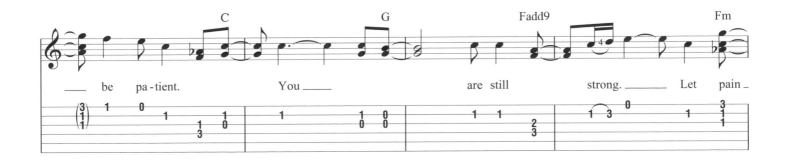

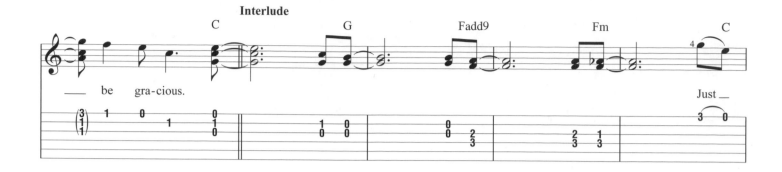

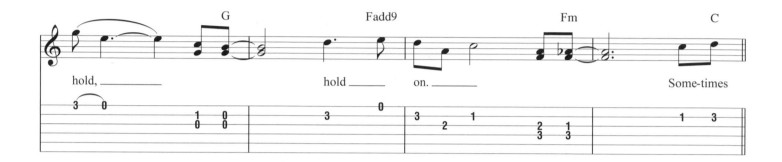

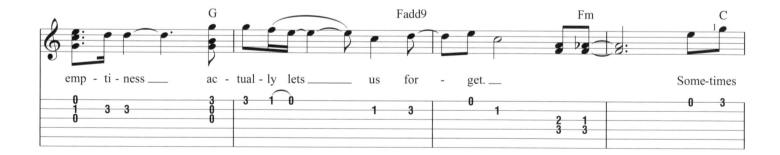

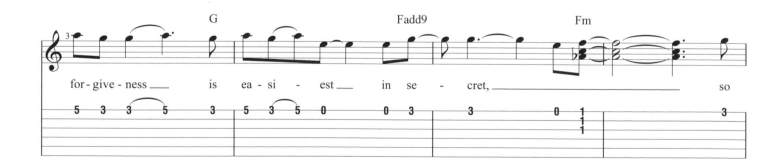

46

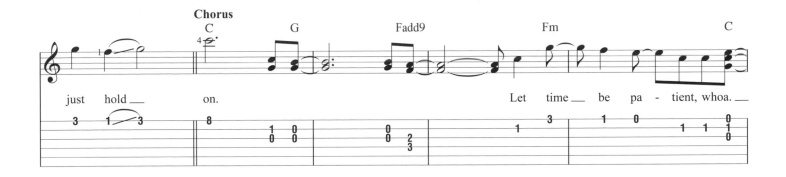

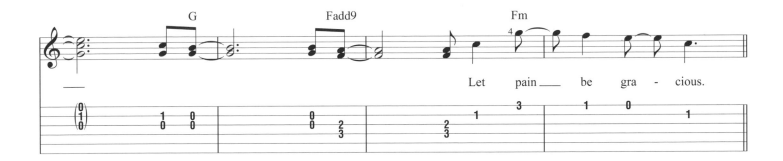

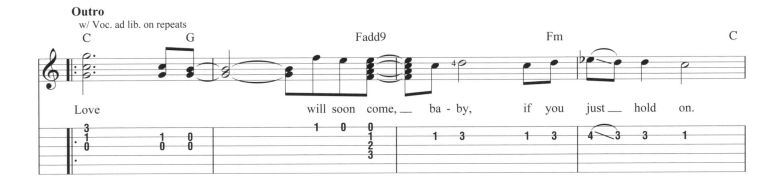

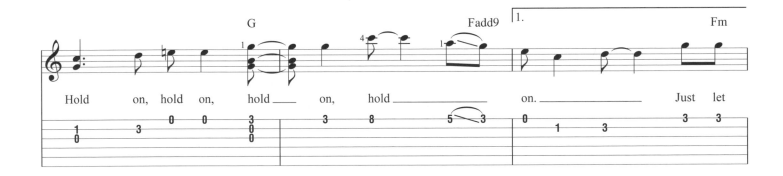

47

TO BE LOVED

WORDS AND MUSIC BY ADELE ADKINS AND TOBIAS JESSO

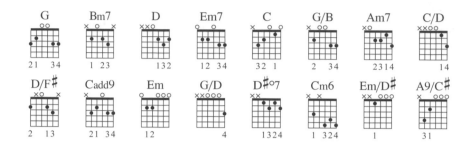

*Capo I

Verse

Slow, freely

1. I built a house for our love to grow, _____ I was so young _____
2. I'm so a-fraid but I'm o - pen wide, _____ I'll be the one _____

*Optional: To match recording, place capo at 1st fret.
**Let chords ring throughout.

_____ that it was hard to know. _ I'm as lost now _____ as I _____ was back then,
_____ to catch my-self this time. _ Try'n' to learn _ to lean in - to it all,

al-ways make a mess of ev-'ry - thing. _____ It's a-bout time that I
ain't it fun-ny how _____ the _____ migh - ty fall? _ Look-ing back _ I don't re -

Pre-Chorus

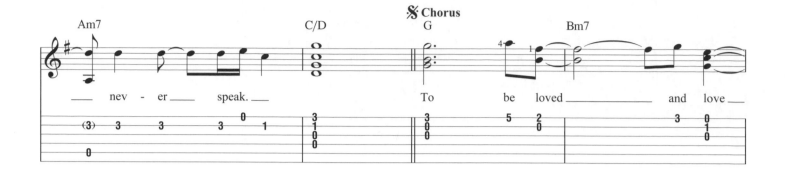

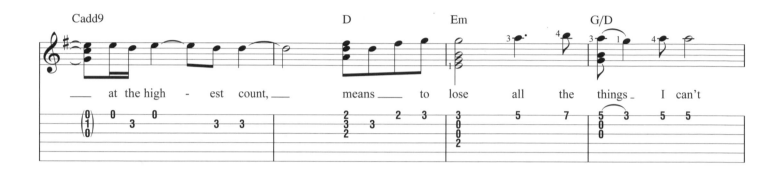

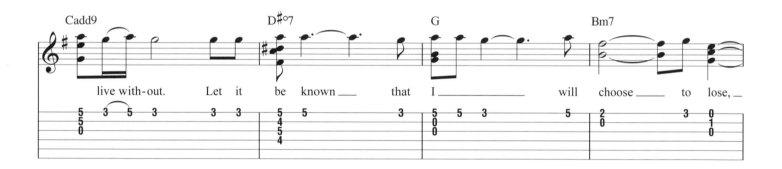

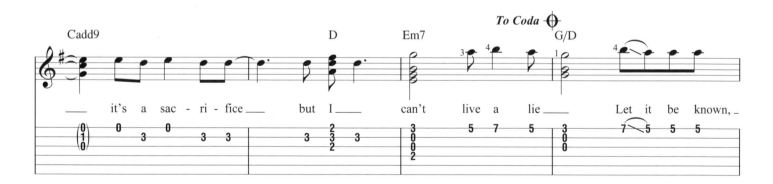

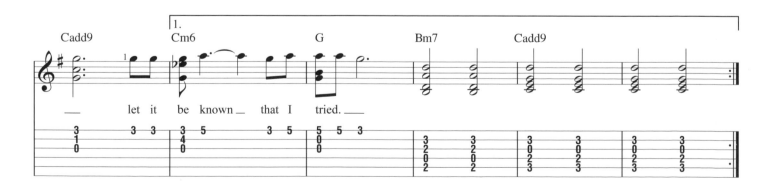

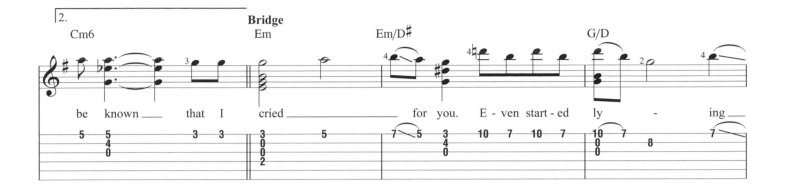

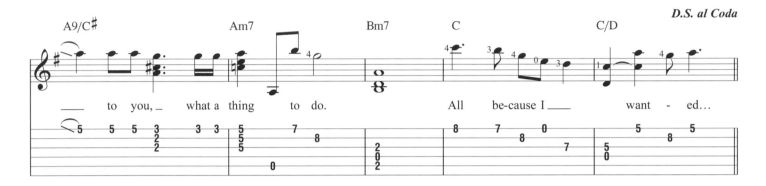

LOVE IS A GAME

WORDS AND MUSIC BY ADELE ADKINS AND DEAN JOSIAH COVER

*Optional: To match recording, place capo at 1st fret.

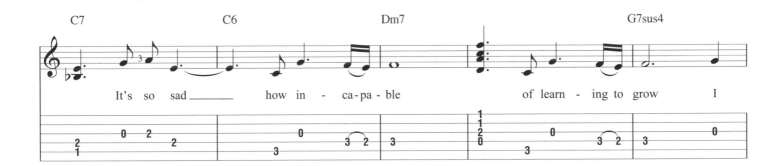

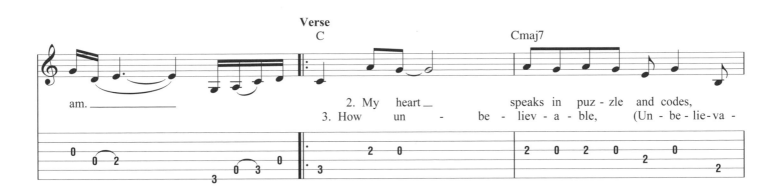

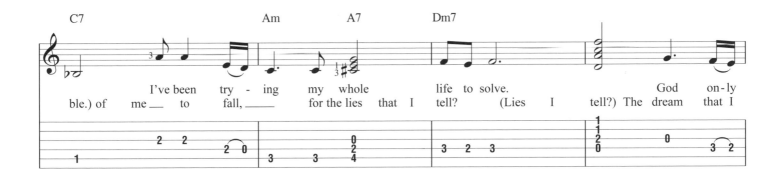

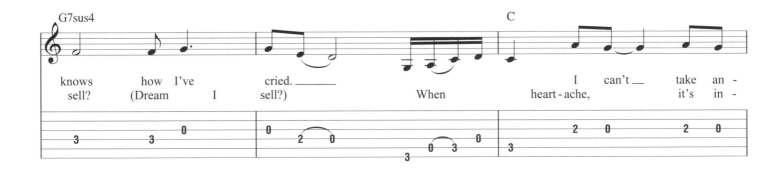

53

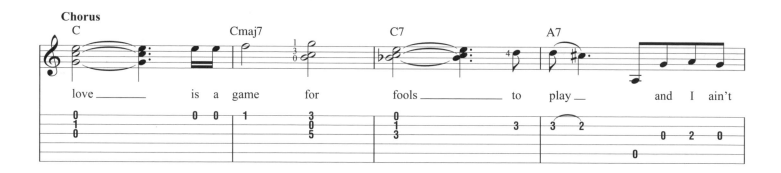

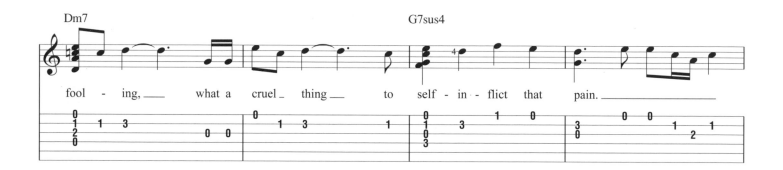

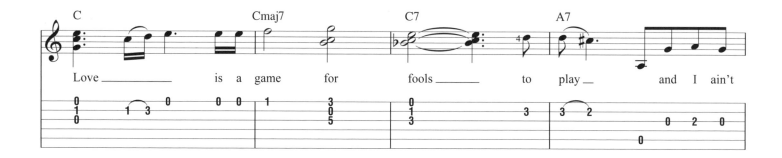

54

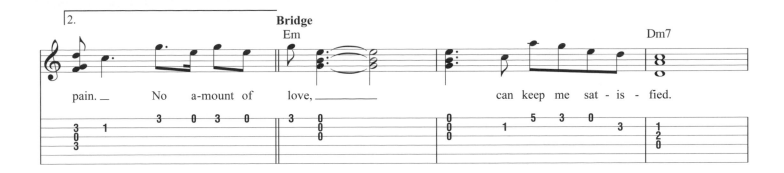

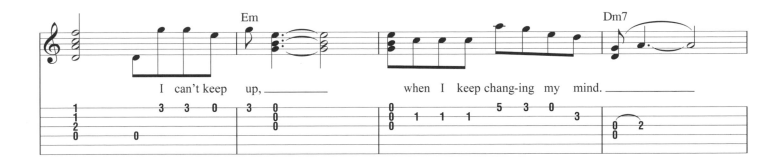

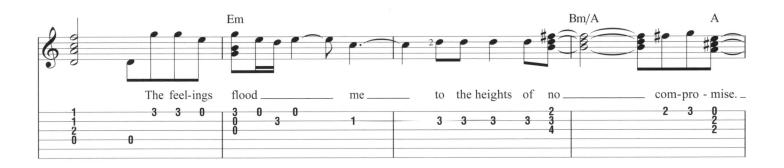

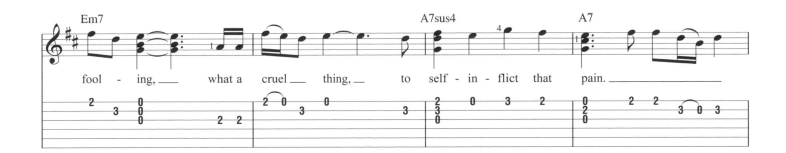

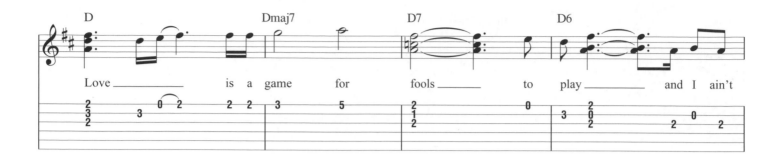

Love _____ is a game for fools _____ to play _____ and I ain't

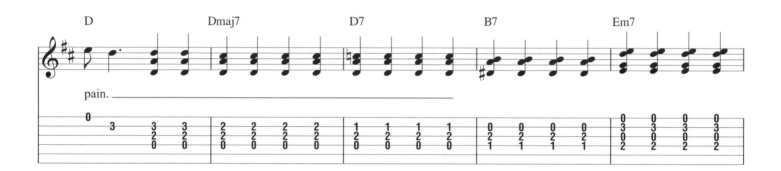

fool - ing _____ what a cruel thing, ___ to self - in - flict that

pain. _____

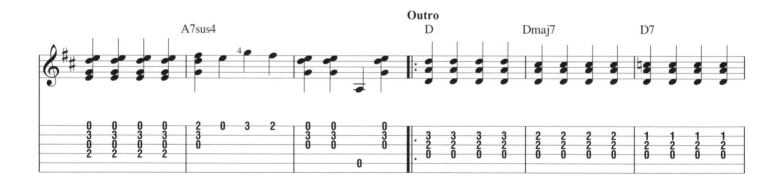

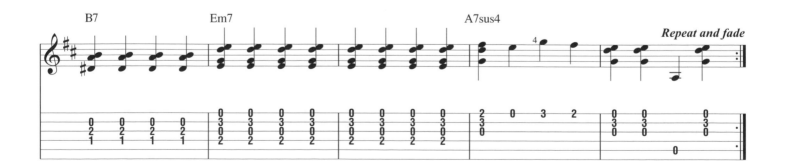